THE GALLERY OF WEST BOHEMIA IN PILSEN

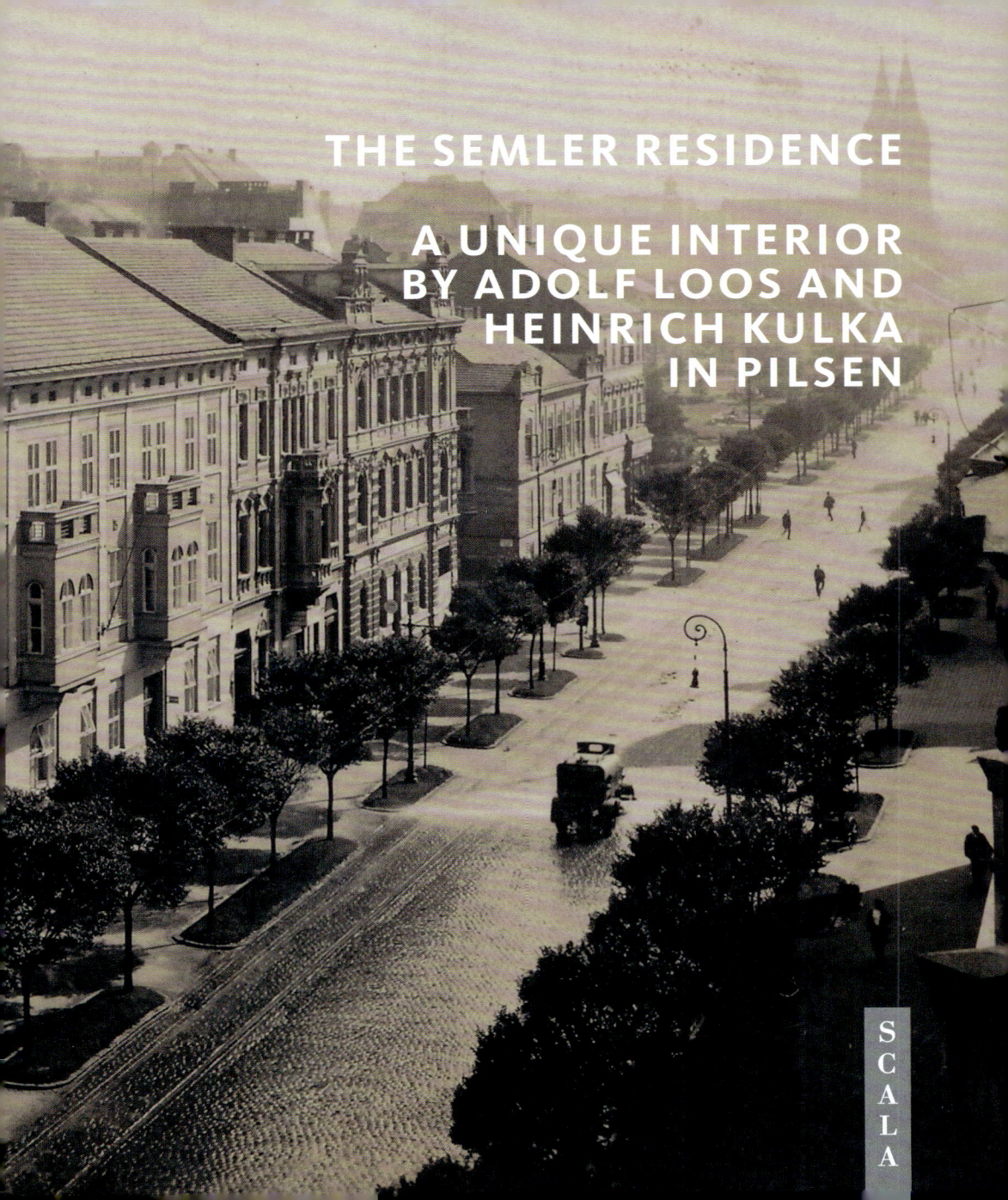

THE SEMLER RESIDENCE

A UNIQUE INTERIOR BY ADOLF LOOS AND HEINRICH KULKA IN PILSEN

CONTENTS

1. Introduction: Adolf Loos – The Path to the Semler Residence   6
   (*Christopher Long*)
2. The 'Adolf Loos Phenomenon' and Pilsen   10
3. The Semler Brothers – Loos's Last Customers in Pilsen   32
4. The Semler Residence – Starring Heinrich Kulka   40
5. The Semler Family and 'Their' Houses after
   the End of the First Czechoslovak Republic   56
6. Restoration of the Semler Residence in 2012–23   64
7. Conclusion   114
8. Select Bibliography   116

1. INTRODUCTION
ADOLF LOOS – THE PATH TO THE SEMLER RESIDENCE

When Oskar and Jana Semler first approached Adolf Loos to renovate their newly purchased apartment building at 110 Klatovská Avenue in Pilsen, he was sixty-one years old and in failing health. The Semlers, who wanted to reconfigure the building and install their own flat in about a third of the structure, adjacent to a large side garden, met with Loos, his assistant Heinrich Kulka and the architect Emil Ondráček, who worked for the local municipality. Also present was Bořivoj Kriegerbeck, who had assisted Loos on several other projects, including an apartment for the families of Leo Brummel and Otto Beck, and the villa of František Müller in Prague. Kriegerbeck later remembered that it was the last time he saw Loos, who died about a year later, on 23 August 1933.

The Semler Residence, which is often described as Loos's last completed commission (despite Kulka's heavy involvement), was a fitting denouement to his career. It is 'Loosian' through and through; his idiosyncratic touches pervade the spaces, even where Kulka's hand is apparent. This is true because Loos was, above all, an architect of *ideas*. He designed and built conceptually, using his many assistants to carry out – to materialise, in the literal sense of the word – his wishes.

When I write that Loos built his thoughts, what I am suggesting is that it is neither the material (the bricks, mortar, wood, concrete and glass) nor the spatial (the framing of the *Raumplan*, Loos's unique strategy of spatial arrangement) that fully defines his works. Loos was always guided instead by the ways in which he envisioned the patterns of daily life: how one should occupy a particular space; how one should move from place to place; how the rooms should be set into hierarchies. He thought of these things before he began to think about walls, rooms or stairs. As his assistants later attested, he would first form a complete concept in his mind before committing anything to paper. In his later years, this work of documenting his thoughts was done almost entirely by his assistants. Loos communicated his wishes to them through verbal description – occasionally supplying a crude rendering or two. The essence of what is 'Loosian' can never be found entirely in this detail or that way of problem solving – even if he was mostly consistent about these things. Each of his houses, apartments and commercial establishments is instead a *meditation* on the needs and rituals of modern life.

Loos's path as an architect can be traced through the ways he confronted and then solved these problems over time. The young Loos, in those first years in Vienna around the turn of the last century, when he began to fashion apartments and shops for friends and acquaintances, was concerned very largely with how modernity could be defined – or, better, how it should be derived. The young Loos rejected the notion that a modern style could be contrived; he was convinced that it arose instead from need and from the traditional crafts. The expert tailor knew what was required for any occasion, just as the consummate cabinetmaker could make a fitting chair or table – pieces that were comfortable and fulfilled the wants of his clients. For most of the first decade and a half after he returned from his sojourn to America, Loos sought to expose these truths. He sought to show not only why a new style was not needed, but also why it made no sense to try to invent it.

From 1909 on, as he began his active career as an architect (he had built very little up to this time), Loos began to investigate how spaces could be framed to facilitate modern living. The villas and shops he designed until the end of the First World War (and, in few cases, a little beyond) were all about how a three-dimensional idea of planning could redeem space that would otherwise be wasted and enhance those rooms that required more height. Loos would continue these explorations for the remainder of his working days. But in the 1920s, he would become far more aggressive in his application of the *Raumplan*. Starting with the Rufer House in 1922, Loos developed increasingly complex (and often, for the occupant, demanding) tactics for organising his spaces. His houses became simple cubes of tightly interlocking volumes on multiple levels. It was only in his last years, after the completion of the Villa Müller in 1930, that he began to forge more relaxed and 'easygoing' spaces.

Much of Loos's work of the early 1920s, however, was about the exigencies of his time. For some five years, from 1919 to 1924, when he headed the Vienna *Siedlungsamt* (municipal housing office), he was occupied with the problem of how to house the largest number of people (the great majority of them working class) as cost-effectively and comfortably as possible. It was largely only after he resigned and moved to Paris in 1924 that Loos once again took up the problems of modern bourgeois living.

The exception to this otherwise neat temporal trajectory, though, was his long engagement with his clients in Pilsen. Loos's work there, if not quite continuous, extended over much of his career. Most of his clients were from the close-knit community of German-speaking Jews. The many apartments that Loos designed in

Pilsen, beginning around 1907 and continuing to the time of his death, were places of comfort and refuge. What Loos understood well about his Pilsen clients was that they wanted to be modern but in a relaxed way. They desired a certain elegance, but not the pretentiousness of, for example, gold-plated water taps. And they wanted places where they could retreat after a long day of work and find peace and cosiness.

What Loos gave his Pilsen clients over the course of these years changed little. He did not believe in 'fast fashion', or the need to be *au courant* at a precise moment. Often his interiors come across as modern, 'without', as the Austrian architect Josef Frank would write, 'one being able to say why'. To us now, these rooms might appear stodgy and gently old-fashioned. This has much to do with Loos's belief that design was an evolutionary process, not a revolutionary one. One should discard only things that no longer had meaning, use or relevance, he thought. Still, that leaves room for a great deal – for older items that remained usable, and, importantly for Loos, for nostalgia. There was no need, he insisted, to cast off pieces from the past simply because they were antique – and that was especially true of objects of real sentimental value.

Loos's many apartments in Vienna, or the handful he designed in Prague or elsewhere, were no different. He thought long and hard about what was 'living', what was current and had a place in modern life. Loos mostly 'designed' by selecting, not inventing. He looked at what was around him, at the products of the best makers, and chose according to what he thought best suited his clients.

When Loos was working as an architect, creating spatial groupings or connected series of rooms, he worked in much the same way. He imagined the quotidian events of the family's existence and gave them form. It is no exaggeration to say that he wrapped these moments of life in bricks and mortar, in concrete and wood; his approach was always immediate and direct.

Given such a way of thinking about design, Loos might have become formulaic. Certainly, when one uses the term 'Loosian', it implies that there is a discernible sameness in his work. Mostly, though, he accomplishes what he does through theme and variation. He picks out what he desires to express or a problem he needs to solve, and often he employs the same answer – or a similar one. This is why Kulka could design in a manner that was decidedly 'Loosian'. He had worked with Loos for so long – going back to the early 1920s – that he could predict Loos's answer to a given problem.

What makes Loos so compelling as a designer, though, is that he was never fully satisfied with his own answers. Throughout his professional life, he kept trying out new ideas, new forms or devices. He continuously re-examined the *Raumplan*, thinking about what could make it work slightly differently or better.

We see this process at work in the Semler Residence. Loos's idea of conjoining a lower space with a higher one goes all the way back to the period around 1907, when he first had his epiphany about how looking out from a theatre box into a larger auditorium made the experience of being in a very low space not only tolerable but visually interesting. The mostly continuous balcony of the Semler Residence is another way of expressing this discovery. But throughout the apartment, Loos compresses or avoids complex spatial planning. He made the space stimulating but kept it liveable. And, above all, he sought to make it cosy (*gemütlich*) and comfortable. Loos's long and winding path that led him eventually to the Semlers and to their flat was a continuous musing on what it meant to be modern and live in a fully modern way.

Christopher Long
University of Texas at Austin

2. THE 'ADOLF LOOS PHENOMENON' AND PILSEN

Adolf Loos holds a very special place among the personalities of European architecture of the late nineteenth century and the first third of the twentieth century. His views and the ways in which he promoted them were unconventional, his methods of designing buildings were unconventional and his private life was also characterised by many peculiarities. The West Bohemian city of Pilsen played an extraordinary role in the life and work of the architect, becoming, after Vienna, the second major focus of his work, paving the way for his most important project in the Czech lands, the Villa Müller in Prague.

Loos was born on 10 December 1870 in the Moravian town of Brno, situated north of Vienna, the capital of the Austro-Hungarian dual monarchy to which the Czech lands then belonged. Adolf's father graduated from the Academy of Fine Arts in Vienna and ran a successful stonemasonry business in Brno. For the young Adolf, the workshop was a dreamland, where he learned a great deal about stonemasonry in his formative years. However, his development was greatly affected by the untimely death of his father when Adolf was less than nine years old. His mother, who now took over the management of the company, planned for Adolf to replace her in the future. However, he did not want to take on this

1/ A detail of the monument erected in 2020 on the site of Loos's birthplace and his father's workshop in Kounicova Street in Brno (sculptor Oldřich Morys and architect Jaroslav Sedlák); photo: Petr Domanický, 2021; ZČG

2/ The Renaissance interior of the so-called lounge hall of the house at 58 Masarykovo Square in Jihlava, where Loos studied, is strikingly reminiscent of the architect's later designs and realisations in its intermingling of adjoining spaces and different height levels; from: PETR, František, and KOSTKA, Jiří, *Městské památkové reservace v Čechách a na Moravě*, Praha 1955

role. After graduating from the Brno School of Industry, he began studying civil engineering at the Technical University in Dresden in 1889, but soon got into trouble through his own negligence, leading to his enlistment in the army. Loos welcomed military service, claiming he felt much freer in the barracks in Vienna than at home. However, the unrestrained lifestyle soon led to debt and illness, which forced him to return home. There he recovered after a few months and was able to return to his studies, but he began to dream of going to America. His mother eventually consented to his plan, but on the condition that he give up the trade and his inheritance.

The three-year stay in the United States marked a major milestone for Loos. As his wife Elsie would later recall in her book *My Life and Adolf Loos*, 'He became enthusiastic about everything that distinguished this country from Austria.' On his return journey to Central Europe, Loos stopped over in Paris and London. Later he revisited both countries several more times, and both the British and American lifestyles were enduring inspirations for him, and the British lifestyle, along with the American one, was one of his enduring inspirations.

In 1896, when Loos was twenty-five years old, he started working in Vienna as an employee of an architectural office. Very soon, however, he also began to develop his own designs. His interest in contemporary culture and fashion led him to design the interiors of apartments and shops in the centre of the capital. Among his early projects, the redesign of the Viennese Café Museum, where he furnished the interior and also designed the new look of the façades of the ground floor, occupies a special place. Following the example of the modern bicycle, which he considered to be the ideal of beauty at the time, he preferred practicality and simplicity, which, with perfect craftsmanship, automatically results in technical elegance. The façade was thus left completely devoid of ornate details. This austerity contrasted sharply not only with the appearance of the historicising buildings in the area, but also with the new exhibition pavilion of the Secession association, built opposite the café's main entrance just a few months earlier. Although Loos agreed with the representatives of the new movement in art on many things, he was bothered by the essential art nouveau maxim, which attempted to subordinate the entire architectural and design work to a single style (the so-called *Gesamtkunstwerk*).

3/ The inglenook as the most important place in a seventeenth-century English house became the forerunner of characteristic resting nooks, including those designed by Loos; drawing: Patricie Císlerová, 2023; ZČG, according to ARTARIA, Paul, *Ferien- und Landhäuser / Weekend- and Country-Houses*, Erlenbach, Zürich 1947, p. 7

Although he was still limited to interior design at the age of thirty and had not yet been given the opportunity to design a house, Loos was becoming well known in and beyond the imperial capital. He capitalised on his strengths. He made use of his talent for observation and, above all, his extraordinary spatial imagination and his use of colours, materials and proportions, as well as his sensitivity to the effect of space on its users. It was as if he had brought a recipe for marketing from America, for he persistently presented his views to the general public and influential individuals.

4/ Adolf Loos, dining room, conservatory and living room in the Hirschs' apartment at 6 Plachého Street, Pilsen, 1908; photo: Josef Hanuš (?), 1930; ZČG

His circle of friends played a crucial role in securing commissions for him. Peter Altenberg and the playwright Karl Kraus (1874–1936) were among his closest allies in the struggle for reforms in culture and art. From 1903 Loos worked on a villa project for the physician Theodor Beer, an associate professor at the University of Vienna, in Clarens, Switzerland. Even in this case, it was not a new building, but it was the first time the architect was given the opportunity to design the exterior of the entire structure, which he created by adding an extension and an addition to another house. He provided it with a flat roof, large windows and smooth façades.

Soon Loos also began to work on his first major works in the Czech lands. These were two residential interiors that were realised between 1907 and 1910 in the

5/ Adolf Loos, view of the main (southern) façade of the 1911 Goldman & Salatsch department store (Looshaus) opposite the Hofburg Palace in Vienna; photo: Karel Lhota (?), c.1926; ZČG

6/ Adolf Loos, mezzanine of the Goldman & Salatsch department store in Vienna, 1909–11; ALBERTINA Museum, Wien, ALA 2425

7/ Adolf Loos, interior of the living room of the villa of Josef and Maria Rufer in Vienna, where the architect first applied his full-fledged spatial design to the representative part of the house in 1922; photo: Bruno Reiffenstein 1922; ALBERTINA Museum, Wien, ALA 2526

West Bohemian town of Pilsen. This expansion of Loos's activities was also closely related to the wider Kraus family. The architect's steps were closely watched by Otto Beck (1868–1936) and his much younger cousin Vilém Hirsch (1886–1941), partners in a major Pilsen wire factory. While Beck had already been reading Loos's texts with enthusiasm, the reason for commissioning the architect was the wedding of Hirsch, Alfred Kraus's brother-in-law, in 1908, and a plan to refurbish an apartment for the newlyweds. Both Hirsches and Becks had their apartments designed by Loos in a single block of flats on Klatovská Avenue – the same block where Emil Škoda, the founder of the region's most important industrial enterprise, had also lived. In addition to Pilsen, Loos subsequently worked also in South Moravia: he designed a villa in Hrušovany near Brno for Viktor Bauer in 1914, and about ten years later he modified a 'chateau' owned by Bauer in his native Brno. Then, of course, he worked again in Pilsen, where he created a unique series of architectural works, which contributed to the subsequent rise of his most famous Prague works.

Already in the first fifteen years of Loos's career, one can see how his distinctive style was forming. It consisted of simple forms, details that were mostly unusual in Central Europe, and especially a particular way of shaping space. Although Loos's contemporaries included several outstanding artists who were simultaneously trying to develop similar influences from the Anglo-American environment, his approach remained in many ways unsurpassed thanks to his flair for integrating seemingly disparate elements into a harmonious whole, and his unique spatial imagination.

Loos is probably the figure most often associated with the ideal of simplicity in form, to which he himself made a significant contribution as early as 1910 with a lecture entitled *Ornament und Verbrechen* (*Ornament and Crime*), adapted from an earlier version, which was later repeated and published.

The Anglo-American environment was responsible for many of the elements Loos preferred. These included characteristic fireplaces, beamed ceilings, resting nooks and sash windows, but also time-honoured period furniture such as Windsor and Chippendale chairs. Loos's continuity with proven classic designs was also evident in the overall design of the living space. Axial symmetry is a typical example. His first idea was to combine the living room with the dining room and various other 'nooks', as was typical of the American family house of the late nineteenth century. From this model he also adopted the combination of living spaces that were mutually interconnected, but screened from the surroundings. He used very high-quality, even luxurious materials and made clever use of various theatrical effects and illusions. He even went so far as to design the buildings from the inside out, so that their façades were largely not the result of thoughtful composition, as is usually the case. The result of his approach was not only the austere volumes of his buildings, but also the surfaces of the façades with irregularly, seemingly randomly placed windows of various formats.

Not only Loos's work but also his everyday life were highly atypical. On the one hand, he saw every incorrect millimetre at work, but on the other hand, his private life was characterised by a certain oddness. He had a need to constantly convince others of his truth, to fight for something, to be a permanent revolutionary and reformer in various fields. Yet, in many ways, his reform consisted of a return to a tried-and-tested tradition.

8/ Adolf Loos, view of the rear (southern) façade of the 1926 Tristan Tzara's house near Montmartre in Paris; photo: Karel Lhota (?), c.1928; ZČG

The year 1910 marked a significant milestone for Loos, as he reached the age of forty, marking an important juncture in his career and architectural endeavours. It was only then that he received several major commissions for new buildings, coming again from the circle of friends for whom he had already worked. For the first time he applied completely smooth façades in the new villa for the textile manufacturer Hugo Steiner and his wife Lilly in Vienna. Soon afterwards (1912–13), Loos built a villa in the same district for the lawyer Gustav Scheu and his wife Helene. Here he also worked with a flat roof and terraced the entire building. Around the same time as the two villas, Loos's most important project was being built: the apartment house and department store of the textile firm Goldman & Salatsch. This building, located directly opposite the Hofburg Palace in the centre of Vienna, was also

9/ A view towards the centre of Pilsen from the south, Klatovská Avenue in the centre, with the synagogue, theatre and St Bartholomew's Church in the back, c.1911; photo: AMP, O 5808

10/ A view from the gallery of the tower of St Bartholomew's Church in Pilsen towards the south-west, on the right the 'great' synagogue and the *Škoda* factory, on the left the city theatre, by which Klatovská Avenue runs southwards (to the left), where the homes of important Pilseners were concentrated, on the bottom left the then brand new house at 28 Republiky Square (the Two Golden Keys house), where Norbert Krieger and, at the turn of 1932–33, also Kulka lived, postcard, *c.*1932; collection (archive) of the author

famous for the smooth façade of the upper part of the building, articulated only by a monotonous grid of windows. The architect also designed the lower part of the building, where the commercial premises were located, in an unusual way: behind the restrained classicising façade and the angled windows, he played out an unusually effective spatial solution, in which rooms of different heights were ingeniously connected by staircases and openings into an almost seamless whole.

Such elements, reminiscent of a theatre stage, became typical for Loos, as did the aforementioned spatial design (called *Raumplan*), which was also related to the theatre and which the architect began to transfer to residential interiors. One of the most important features was the height difference in the various spaces and their simultaneous interconnection, complementing the enclosure of the interior from the outside world.

11/ Adolf Loos in a garden restaurant near Pilsen during a consultation with clients, 1930; LA ML-PNP

However, even the popularity that Loos gained from the various scandals associated with his texts, lectures and new buildings did not help him to secure the large commissions he dreamed of. His first major private building on an important site, the aforementioned department store, was also his last, and the focal point of his work remained in residential interiors and family houses.

In 1922, Loos came up with a prototype of a *Raumplan* for a residential interior in the Viennese villa of the merchant Josef Rufer and his wife Maria, which he then developed over the next decade. The central space of the apartment occupied almost the entire area of the lower part of the house. It consisted mainly of a large lounge, which was adjoined by a partly hidden access from the main entrance, as well as a staircase, with a dining room on the mezzanine floor, located somewhat above the lounge but forming a single unit with it.

Alongside his experiments with *Raumplan* in luxurious Viennese family houses and other designs for apartments in the centre of Vienna, Loos also worked again after the First World War at his private building school, which he had founded before the war. He was also given another opportunity at that time when he was appointed to a senior position in the *Siedlungsamt* – an office managing the construction of social housing. He took part in an international competition for an office building for the *Chicago Tribune* in Chicago and, among other things, designed sets of houses, a town hall for Mexico City, a hotel in Zagreb and the tiered Grand Hotel Babylon in Nice. Nonetheless there were no major commissions for public

THE SEMLER RESIDENCE | **19**

12/ The living room in the apartment of the Beck family, originally built by Loos at 12 Klatovská Avenue, Pilsen, in 1910; here, after the interior was transferred to the Müller family house at 2 Míru Square and modified (e.g. by adding a fireplace) by Loos in 1928–29; photo: Josef Hanuš (?), 1930; ZČG

13/ Hedvika Liebstein's living rooms, realised by Loos in 1930 at 58 Husova Avenue, Pilsen, as part of a two-generation apartment shared with the Brummels; photo: Radovan Kodera, 2016; ZČG

14/ The promotional photograph of the *Škoda Sentinel* steam sprinkler car shows the Brummel couple's house at 58 Husova Avenue, Pilsen (in the background), which Loos designed with the assistance of Karel Lhota; photo: 1929; SOA v Plzni, office Klášter, fund Škoda Plzeň, photographic documentation, 33-178

15/ A model of the house at 6 Plachého Street, Pilsen, with a reconstruction of the unpreserved apartment of Vilém and Marta Hirsch, designed by Loos in 1908 and completed in 1927–30 by Loos and Lhota (boudoir and conservatory on the right); model: Miroslav Koranda, 2011; ZČG, photo: Oto Palán, 2012

buildings and Loos remained focused mainly on housing and shopfitting. In 1924 he decided to leave Vienna permanently and move to Paris. Yet even there, the situation did not improve. His most important Paris project was a house for Tristan Tzara, a versatile artist and collector originally from Romania, whose nonconformist attitudes towards society were not unlike those of Karl Kraus and Loos himself. In the project, carried out in 1926 near Montmartre, Loos revisited his Viennese vision of terrace houses and the concept of Josef Rufer's house.

Loos did not work continuously in France. Simultaneously, he strengthened his ties to the young Czechoslovak Republic, whose passport he used during his travels through Europe. As the text promoting Loos's lectures held in 1925 in Prague and Brno recalled with certain exaggeration, the architect was in fact a 'Czechoslovak Anglo-French American' living at the time on the express London–Paris–Vienna–Brno–Prague and back.

The fact that he became acquainted with the art aesthetician and teacher Bohumil Markalous (also known as Jaromír John) and, through him, with the architect Karel Lhota, was of great importance for Loos's further activities in Czechoslovakia. In 1927 the owner of a textile factory, Hans Moller, and his wife Anny commissioned him to design their villa in Vienna, and he was also approached with more work by clients he had already worked with in Pilsen; therefore the architect returned to Central Europe, contrary to his earlier plans. Vienna and Pilsen then remained the focal points of his work, to which, through his circle of Pilsen clients, several commissions in Prague – including the greatest one, the Villa

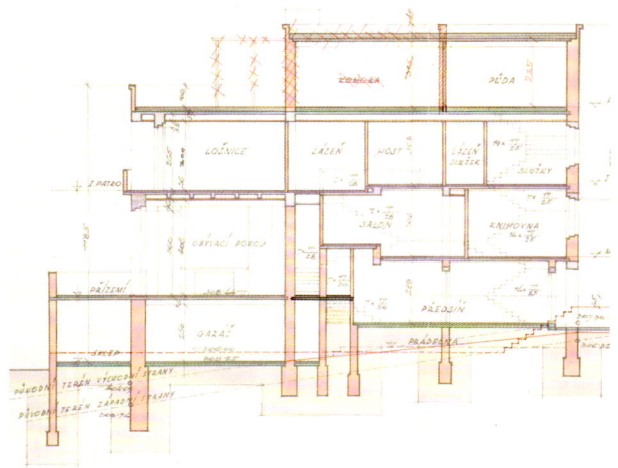

16/ A cross-section of the Villa Müller, designed by Adolf Loos and Karel Lhota, in Prague and built by Kapsa & Müller building company in November 1928, showing the different heights of the significant spaces and their interconnections; photo: UPM

17/ A view of the Villa Müller at 14 Nad hradním vodojem Street in Prague-Střešovice from the north-east shortly before its completion, 1929; photo: UPM

Müller – were added, as if in lieu of the desired but unrealised major buildings in Paris and elsewhere. Loos offered Lhota, who had been teaching at the industrial school in Pilsen since 1925, to work for his clients there. Together they extended the apartment of the family of Vilém and Marta Hirsch and worked on relocating the apartment of the family of Otto and Olga Beck. The two were then joined by Jan (Hanuš) Brummel (1892–1960), who had Loos renovate and extend the house on Husova Avenue where the apartment of Jan and Jana Brummel and Hedvika Liebsteinová, Brummel's mother-in-law, was located. In turn, Lhota approached Loos to design a new villa in Prague for František and Milada Müller. The couple came from Pilsen and it was there that the studies and the detailed design of the villa were created. It was of considerable significance both in Loos's work and in the development of architecture in Czechoslovakia as a whole, as it was the first time that the architect had implemented his spatial design of a residential interior on such a large scale in this country. The related spaces were not only related to

18/ A view from the living hall to the dining room (left) and entrance in the Villa Müller in Prague, illustrating the extraordinary structural complexity of Loos's *Raumplan*; photo: Atelier Pařík a spol., 1929; UPM

19/ František Müller's room in the Villa Müller in Prague immediately after completion, 1930; the solution of many elements and the choice of materials as well as various ideas are strongly reminiscent of the interior subsequently created in the Semler Residence in Pilsen; photo: UPM

20/ Adolf Loos, Heinrich Kulka, the living hall in the 1930 Paul Khuner's house (Landhaus) in Payerbach (on the foothill of the Alps, south-west of Vienna); also in this case many elements resemble or coincide with the later Semler Residence; photo: Martin Gerlach Jr, 1929–30; ALBERTINA Museum, Wien, ALA 2289

each other, but also intertwined in all three directions. Loos himself said that the spaces needed to be connected so that the transition was almost imperceptible. He claimed, somewhat brazenly, that while for him this principle was self-evident, for others it remained a mystery.

Although the second most important source of Adolf Loos's work after Vienna was already established in Pilsen before the First World War, his work was long known in Bohemia only by insiders and especially architects, apart from the families of investors. Loos became more widely known in Bohemia only in the period shortly before 1930. The activities of Bohumil Markalous and Karel Lhota were also important in the popularisation of the architect's work at that time. The former initiated the publication of the Czech translation of Loos's *Ins Leere gesprochen* (1897–1900; published in English as *Spoken into the Void*, 1982), to which Lhota also contributed. Another of Loos's important collaborators, Heinrich (Henry) Kulka (1900–71), prepared a book on Loos at that time and published it the following year in Vienna with the first comprehensive overview of his work. In addition to the Villa Müller, he rounded it off with another novelty, which was Paul Khuner's mountain villa (*Landhaus*) in

21/ Adolf Loos, Heinrich Kulka, view from the south-east of one of the two 1932 semi-detached houses in the *Werkbund* housing estate in Vienna; photo: Petr Domanický, 2022; ZČG

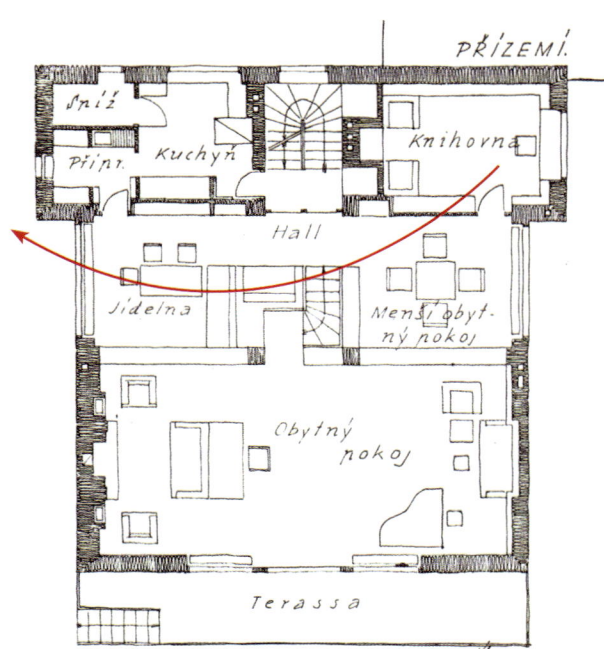

22/ Adolf Loos, Karel Lhota, floorplan diagram of the representative part of the Villa Winternitz completed in 1932 at 10 Na Cihlářce Street, Prague-Smíchov; its layout with a dining room and living space located on the gallery of the living hall represents a transition in the use of Loos's *Raumplan* between the Villa Müller and the Semler Residence (the arrow shows the position of the rooms in the Semler residence); from URBAN, Bohumil Stanislav and FELIX, Adolf (eds), *SV. 34: Sborník výtvarného umění*, Praha, 1934, p. 83, ZČG

Payerbach, south-west of Vienna. It was Kulka who worked with Loos on the project, whose importance was crucial, among other things, for the final form of the Semler Residence. He came from the Moravian town of Litovel, where his father Mořic Kulka had a textile shop. After the First World War, Heinrich studied architecture at the Technical University in Vienna, but did not complete his studies. At the same time, he was educated privately at a school run by Loos. As a draughtsman, he also worked on his teacher's projects, so that he was, for example, present at the designing of the Rufer House, where Loos first applied a prototype of his *Raumplan*. Later, Kulka became Loos's collaborator and was also his key promoter and was involved in the preservation of documents from Loos's Vienna office.

After mid-July 1929 Loos's connection to Pilsen deepened even further, as the twenty-four-year-old Claire (Klára) Becková (1904–42), daughter of the architect's loyal customer Otto Beck, became his third wife. In addition to the celebration of Loos's sixtieth birthday (which took place in the Villa Müller), one of their major experiences together was a journey through Europe lasting many months. In the

25/ The wedding of Adolf Loos to Claire (Klára) Beck in July 1929; to the right of Loos are Heinrich Kulka and Olga Beck; drawing: Patricie Císlerová, 2023; ZČG, based on a photo by Trude Fleischmann

spring and summer of 1931 they travelled through Italy and Switzerland, and stayed in Paris and also in the south of France. Loos worked there too, but he did not win any major commission even there. His marriage to Claire (Klára) did not last long and ended the same year.

Loos never got the opportunity to design the great buildings of his dreams, in Western Europe or elsewhere, and the very end of his life was no exception. Only his projects for family houses in Vienna, Prague and several apartments in Pilsen (in addition to those he designed before the war) were carried out. In Prague, the Villa Winternitz was built according to Loos and Karel Lhota's design, and, this time in cooperation with Kulka, Loos prepared the construction of two similar semi-detached houses, built in 1932 in the exemplary housing colony organised by the local *Werkbund* (German Association of Craftsmen) and the Viennese municipality. After the construction of the Villa Müller, Loos collaborated on a number of his creative ideas and plans with the Pilsen construction company Müller & Kapsa (or Kapsa & Müller, its sister company operating in Prague), which was managed by František Müller. However, few of the designs were executed. Except for minor modifications to the Kapsas' villa, none of the projects described came to fruition at the time. Only the project of the family of Oskar Semler (1882–1961) and his wife Jana (Hanna, Hanne, Jane; 1898–1992) in Pilsen eventually saw the light of day.

24/ The tombstone of Otto Beck and his daughter Eva Schanzer at the 'new' Jewish cemetery on Rokycanská Avenue in Pilsen; photo: Petr Domanický, 2022; ZČG

25/ A Detail of the cover of Heinrich Kulka's 1931 book on Loos; SVK PK; photo: Petr Domanický; ZČG

3. THE SEMLER BROTHERS – LOOS'S LAST CUSTOMERS IN PILSEN

As in many other large cities in Central Europe, one of Pilsen's most interesting periods in modern history was the era around 1900. The Czech population was getting a decisive say in the running of the city over the German citizens, and Pilsen was becoming one of the important centres not only in the Czech lands, but also in the whole Austro-Hungarian monarchy. The unique location of Pilsen played a role in this, and in a short period between 1861 and 1870 it became the crossroads of the railway lines connecting Vienna and Prague with Bavaria, with other directions soon following. The city began to transform into one of the most important centres of industry in Central Europe, especially in the fields of metal-working and beer production. In a short period of time, a modern Joint-Stock Brewery complex was built next to the existing Burghers' Brewery, and Emil Škoda bought a small machine shop in the city, to which he soon added a foundry, and then began to build a completely new factory complex on another site, with its products soon achieving widespread fame. The important industrial enterprises in Pilsen focused on metal production also included wire and nail factories. The first of them was established as early as 1863, and less than a decade later, another was built by Carl Tuschner and Richard Hirsch. In the 1890s, Šimon (Simon) Semler (1852–1921) also entered into the metalworking business.

26/ A detail of the tombstone of Šimon and Berta Semler from the early 1920s (probably designed by the architect Adolf Hrussa) in the 'new' Jewish cemetery on Rokycanská Avenue in Pilsen; photo: Radovan Kodera, 2011; ZČG

27/ The family of Šimon and Berta Semler, son Oskar on the left, Hugo on the right; photo: Atelier Carl Pietzner, *c.*1905; ZČM, NO, NMP 63774

In this context, it is worth mentioning that both Hirsch and Semler were Jewish, and that Jewish entrepreneurs had a significant share in the development of Pilsen in general. Jews had lived in Pilsen more or less since its foundation in the Middle Ages (*c.*1295), but at the beginning of the sixteenth century they were expelled from the city (as elsewhere in Bohemia). Their gradual return and equalisation was only brought about by the social changes of the late eighteenth century and the years 1848 and 1867. In 1870 more than 1,200 Jewish people were among the 22,000 inhabitants of Pilsen. At the beginning of the 1890s a new synagogue was built, one of the largest in Europe.

29/ Situation of the so-called 'Red Mill' (Červený mlýn) in Vochov near Pilsen with a drawing of the new building of Šimon Semler's wire factory, 1900; *G-Team Holding SE*, Vochov plant

28/ Advertisement of Šimon Semler's factories; from: SCHIEBL Jaroslav, *Adressář král města Plzně 1897*, Plzeň, 1897; AMP

When Richard Hirsch and his wife Sidonie died at the beginning of the twentieth century, their son Vilém, then only seventeen years old, became the owner of the Hirsch factory. His older cousin Otto Beck, who later became Hirsch's partner in the company, was also involved in the management of the company. Both men have already been mentioned in connection with the first of Loos's designs in Pilsen.

While the focus of Hirsch's production was essentially unchanged from the beginning, Šimon Semler's interests gradually evolved until they settled on the production of metal elements. First, in 1881, he set up a shop in Pilsen selling dried fruit, pulses, firewood and coal. He then took the first step towards the production of his own metal goods by taking over the hammer mill in Chrást near Pilsen from his father-in-law Moritz Klauber. After modernising the mill he set up a factory for the production of farm tools. In 1892 he acquired another hammer mill in neighbouring Nová Huť (part of Dýšina), and at the end of the century, crucially for the future development of the company, he bought the Červený mlýn (Red Mill) in Vochov, also near Pilsen, only on the opposite side. On the site of the mill he built a modern two-storey building, which was then used for the production of wire and nails.

In 1911, ten years after the start of production, Semler's eldest sons Hugo (1881–1960) and Oskar (1882–1961), contemporaries of Vilém Hirsch, became his partners. While Hugo was engaged in the timber trade, his younger brother, a graduate in mechanical engineering from the Technical University in Dresden, was instrumental in the further development of the metalworking part of the company. Not only did Oskar Semler mastermind the gradual expansion of the range of goods made from wire and thus the development of the Vochov site, but

30/ Šimon Semler's factory in Vochov, with the oldest production building at the back, c.1915; AMP, collection of photographs, O 4361

31/ Joint advertising for wire mesh by R. Hirsch and Š. Semler companies; from: *Pestrý týden* XI, 11 July 1936, p. 21

he also initiated the ambitious solution to the problem of the supply of the raw materials. The Semlers and Hirschs, together with several other entrepreneurs from Pilsen and Žatec, built a large steelworks and wire-rolling mill in Most, North Bohemia, between 1914 and 1916. When the founder of the Semler factory, Šimon Semler, retired before the end of 1920, the family business was taken over by the sons themselves. The range of wire products gradually expanded to include, for example, wire for umbrellas and spokes for bicycles, as well as needlework goods, including pins, knitting needles, safety pins and many other items. From 1927 Semler's company added gramophone needles to its production; these soon gained popularity and were exported to many European countries and also to North Africa. It also continued to produce farm tools such as axes, hoes and plough parts, and tools for carpenters and masons. Based on a licence from a company in Luxembourg, Semler, Hirsch and others introduced the production of special concrete reinforcement bars called ISTEG in Most in the late 1920s; this technology soon found application in a number of important buildings throughout the country due to its cost-effectiveness.

The two businessmen, Richard Hirsch and Šimon Semler, bought houses only a few dozen metres apart in 1897–8, at the best address in Pilsen at that time, near the intersection of Americká and Klatovská Avenues. As mentioned above, in 1907–10, the then partners of the Hirsch factory had their apartments in this location furnished according to the designs of Adolf Loos. The Semler brothers also had the Semler family's house at 19 Klatovská Avenue modernised in the mid-1920s, originally according to a design by the Pilsen architect Adolf Hrussa, a renowned professor at the local German technical school. The entire ground floor and part of

32/ Boxes for pins, sewing accessories and record-player styluses produced by *Šimon Semler* company in the 1930s; collection (archive) of the author; photo: Petr Domanický, 2023; ZČG

33/ A detail of a pin box made under the *Sem* brand in the 1950s; collection (archive) of the author; photo: Petr Domanický, 2023; ZČG

the basement were converted into the company's headquarters. On the first floor, where Hugo's family lived, several of the most important rooms were given a luxury appearance. After 1930 they approached Loos, who designed further modifications to the house. The impetus for commissioning the famous architect was probably, among other things, the recommendation of Vilém Hirsch (or perhaps his wife Marta). The intercession of Klára (Claire) Becková, who had been Loos's wife since 1929, may also have played a part. Most likely, the fresh experience with the newly completed rooms that the Hirschs, Becks, Brummels and others had adapted to Loos's designs in their apartments in 1927–30 was equally as important.

34/ Production of thin wire in *Š. Semler* plant in Vochov, *c.*1938; collection (archive) of Vilém (Will) Semler

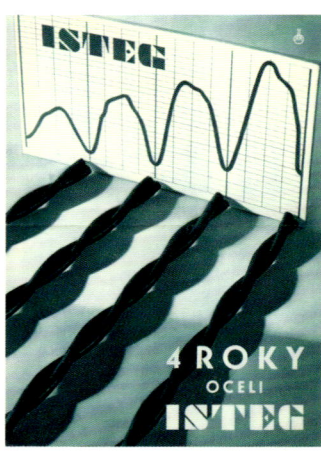

35/ Advertising leaflet for ISTEG rebar manufactured in Most, *c.*1935; collection (archive) of the author

36/ The Semlers with their sons Vilém, Štěpán and Oldřich in 1927; collection (archive) of Vilém (Will) Semler

4. THE SEMLER RESIDENCE – STARRING HEINRICH KULKA

During the renovations at 19 Klatovská Avenue, the Semlers first had Loos create a new look for only one room, which was the 'music salon' in Hugo and Helena's apartment. It was located on the first floor and was largely redecorated by Hrussa. Loos's interior, realised in the early months of 1932, was co-designed by Norbert Krieger (1901–82), who had previously attended Loos's classes in Vienna. From the autumn of 1930 he worked in the Pilsen joinery firm of Jan Mráček, which furnished Loos-designed interiors in Pilsen, including the Semlers'. In conjunction with the room, Loos worked on a commission for the Semlers that was quite extraordinary in comparison to his other Pilsen works. It was a design for an extension of the aforementioned house, where (probably in collaboration with Mráček) a very large apartment was to be built for the family of the younger Semler brother, Oskar. In the spring of 1932 Loos prepared two variants of the extension in collaboration with Krieger and Ulrich Straub, who had also worked for him since September 1928. As we know, Heinrich Kulka was also significantly involved in the project at that time. While in the first variant we can recognise an attempt to draw a more lavish parallel to the one-level apartment that the Semlers knew from Marta and Vilém Hirsch, in the second variant they scaled their vision much more ambitiously, following the spatial concept of Prague's Villa Müller and the Parisian house of Tristan Tzara.

Loos came up with a solution based on the principles of *Raumplan*, utilising it for the first time in Pilsen in his quarter of a century of working here, at a time when his similarly spatially conceived villa for Josef and Jenny Winternitz was being built in Prague. The central space of the Semlers' apartment was to become a lounge almost two storeys high. The apartment was to have a total of seven levels of height, with the roof terrace forming the eighth level.

As the original house had been rebuilt several times in the past, the planned extension would be technically and structurally very demanding and therefore very expensive. Based on these complications, the Semlers decided to abandon their intention to establish their home in the house where other family members lived and where the company headquarters were located. However, they did not abandon the grandiose concept of the apartment, outlined in the plans from early June 1932; on the contrary, they developed them further. They found another building that

37/ The 'marble' music room designed by Loos in the apartment of Hugo and Helena Semler at 19 Klatovská Avenue, Pilsen, connected to the rooms previously designed by architect Adolf Hrussa; photo: Radovan Kodera, 2011; ZČG

allowed them to incorporate the intended apartment, at number 110 on the same avenue. Although it was located about three-quarters of a mile further south and therefore outside the city centre (in the suburb of Bory), it was still in close proximity to the homes of a number of prominent families close to the Semlers. In this context, it is worth recalling that Klatovská Avenue had been an important social axis of Pilsen since well before the First World War, in the vicinity of which were concentrated, among other things, important institutions, shops and the homes of important families and personalities.

38/ A view along Klatovská Avenue towards the historical centre of Pilsen, with number 19 in the middle of the row on the right, the synagogue on the left at the back, c.1928; ZČM, OND, NB 90–17

Relatively little is known about the beginnings of the Semlers' apartment project on the new site, and the reports are also blurred by inconsistencies. What is certain is that the Semlers officially bought the house before the end of 1932 and at the beginning of the following year Heinrich Kulka drew up a project of modifications, the main part of which was the construction of an atypical apartment. In many sources, this apartment, realised between 1933 and 1934, is considered to be Loos's work, at least in its spatial concept. This information has been primarily based on the testimony of Bořivoj Kriegerbeck, an employee of the design and construction firm Müller & Kapsa, whose headquarters were located near the construction site and which also carried out the renovations on the apartment. Kriegerbeck, who had recently been involved in the construction of his boss František Müller's Prague villa, recollected a meeting at which the design of the Semlers' apartment was discussed in Loos's presence. The problem is that the event cannot be clearly dated, and what is more, Kulka eventually began to present the whole work as exclusively his own. Soon after its completion, the Austrian cultural magazine *Die Bühne* also presented it in a curious way, saying that Kulka had worked at the Semlers' 'in the spirit of Loos'. Almost at the same time, this pupil and collaborator of Loos designed a villa for Alfréd Kantor in Jablonec nad Nisou, North Bohemia, which shows some similarities with the Pilsen apartment. Kulka also recalled his collaboration in two projects where he was still a co-author at the end of Loos's life, which closely preceded the Semlers' apartment. Loos's creative activity was already declining at the time, and the exact ratio of the contribution

39/ A model of 19 Klatovská Avenue, Pilsen, with the unrealised extension of the apartment of Oskar Semler's family according to the second version of Adolf Loos's design from June 1932, view from the street; model: Miroslav Koranda, 2022; ZČG; photo: Karel Kocourek, 2022; ZČG

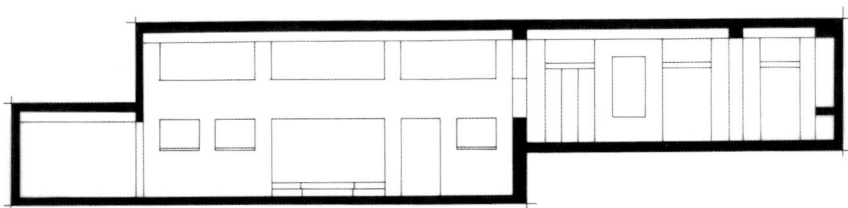

40/ A cross-section of the lounge in the apartment of Oskar Semler's family in the planned extension of 19 Klatovská Avenue according to the second version of Loos's design from June 1932; on the right is the elevated dining room, on the left the resting nook, another one is below the gallery. The overall concept is strongly reminiscent of the subsequently realised interior at 110 Klatovská Avenue; drawing: Petr Domanický, 2022; ZČG; based on LONG, Christopher, *Adolf Loos: Poslední domy / The Last Houses*, Praha 2020, p. 154

of the two architects in these cases is thus difficult to determine. Although we have similar reports from other buildings by Loos, we assume that while he was still able to work, Loos would hardly have had someone else solve the spatial concept for him: he had devised the *Raumplan* principle himself, was proud of it and was unsurpassed in executing it.

We know that from June 1932, the Semler family intended to acquire an apartment designed by Loos that was geared towards a generous spatial project involving the *Raumplan* principle. Although they had to abandon the earlier project devised by Loos, it is logical and highly probable that even then they sought to modify the plan for the newly acquired house with the same architect. This is consistent with the aforementioned testimony of Bořivoj Kriegerbeck about the negotiations involving both Kulka and Loos, who was staying near Pilsen at the time and trying to work when he could. At the meeting in Pilsen, which took place sometime between the end of September and the beginning of November 1932, besides the investors and architects, representatives of the building company and the building authorities were also present. It can thus be assumed that at least the rough outlines of the modified concept must have been set by then. The actual form of these outlines is unknown as Loos used to clarify his spatial ideas quickly and communicate them mainly orally and through various simple sketches to his collaborators. But then Loos left for Vienna, where he had to stay in a boarding house because he could no longer climb the stairs to his apartment. Apparently as a result of the strenuous journey, he had suffered a stroke and subsequently stayed in the Rosenhügel sanatorium and was confined to a wheelchair. In June 1933 Loos was transferred to a sanatorium in Kalksburg near Vienna, and he died on 23 August that year.

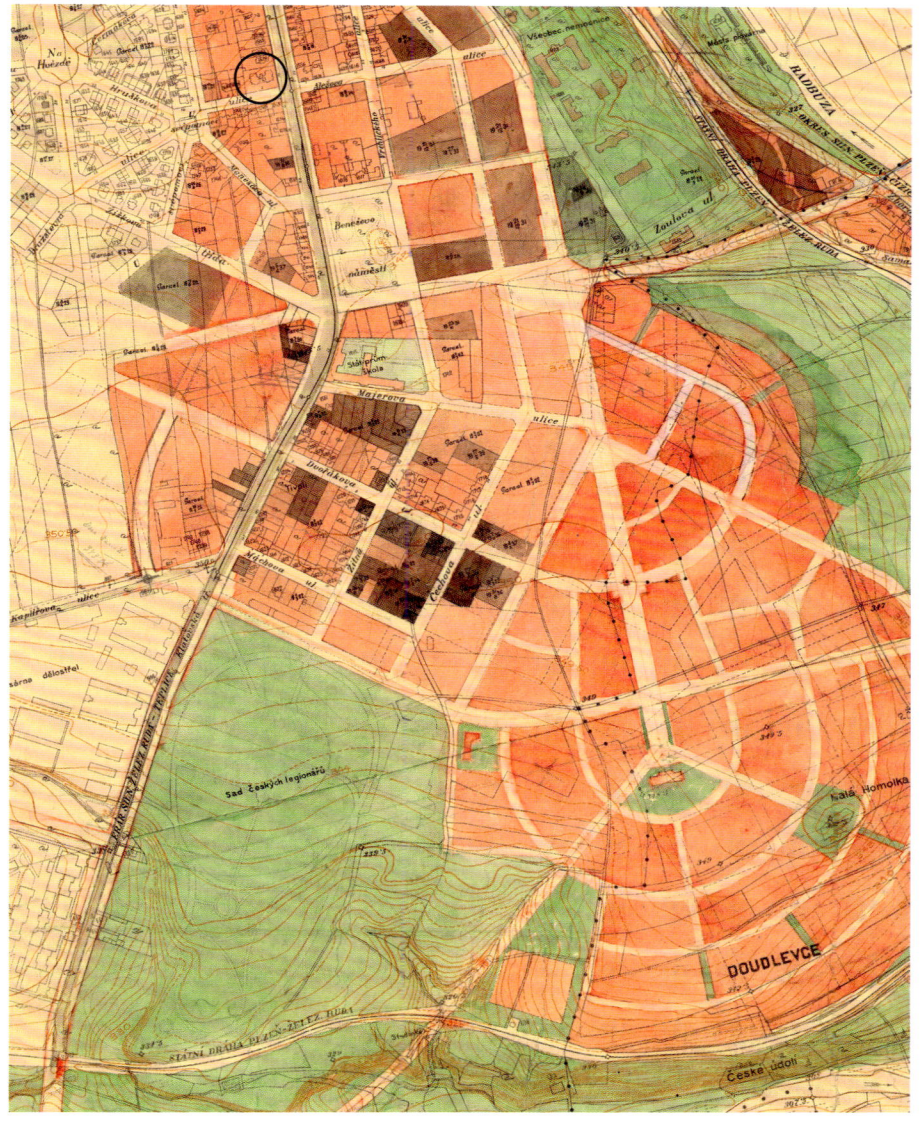

41/ A cut-out from a design by urban planner Vladimír Zákrejs for a mostly unrealised solution of the future form of the Bory district in Pilsen from the first half of the 1930s, with Klatovská Avenue on the left and the location of number 110 marked on it; AMP, maps and plans collection, M 2741/1

42/ 110 Klatovská Avenue before adaptation for the Semler family; SOA v Plzni, Office Klášter, fund Škoda Plzeň, Photographic Documentation, 71–425

43/ An inscription dating the building of 110 Klatovská Avenue, Pilsen, was found on the inner side of the plinth of a light fixture located at the staircase; photo: Petr Domanický, 2016; ZČG

The design, preserved in the collection of Vienna's ALBERTINA Museum, was prepared for the Semlers in 1933 by Kulka himself due to Loos's deteriorating health, and was executed with the assistance of Krieger, without the usual consultations with Loos. Kulka probably based the design on Loos's spatial concept, and certainly on plans that he had probably sketched for the previous site a little earlier under Loos's instructions (and possibly with some input from himself). The core of the whole spatial concept is strikingly similar (although influenced in implementation by the conditions of the new building site) – a high lounge with an adjoining raised dining room, resting nooks and a gallery with a pair of pillars. It is also important to note that, in many aspects, Kulka complied with the wishes of the investors, who wanted 'a Loos interior' from the beginning. The entire space is thus very 'Loosian', strongly reminiscent in its concept of the Villa Müller in Prague: it is very different from buildings designed by Kulka from scratch (including the aforementioned Villa Kantor), and closely connected to many other Loos's works (such as Tzara's house in Paris, Villa Moller in Vienna and Landhaus Khuner) not only by common principles, but also by numerous similar or even identical details.

Taking these findings into account, being aware of Loos's exceptional design practices and acknowledging Heinrich Kulka's major contribution to the final realisation, we certainly do not want to claim that the latter 'merely' copied Loos in the main essence and details. At the same time, however, there is no reason to distrust Kriegerbeck's report, and it seems logical that the Semlers would have checked in

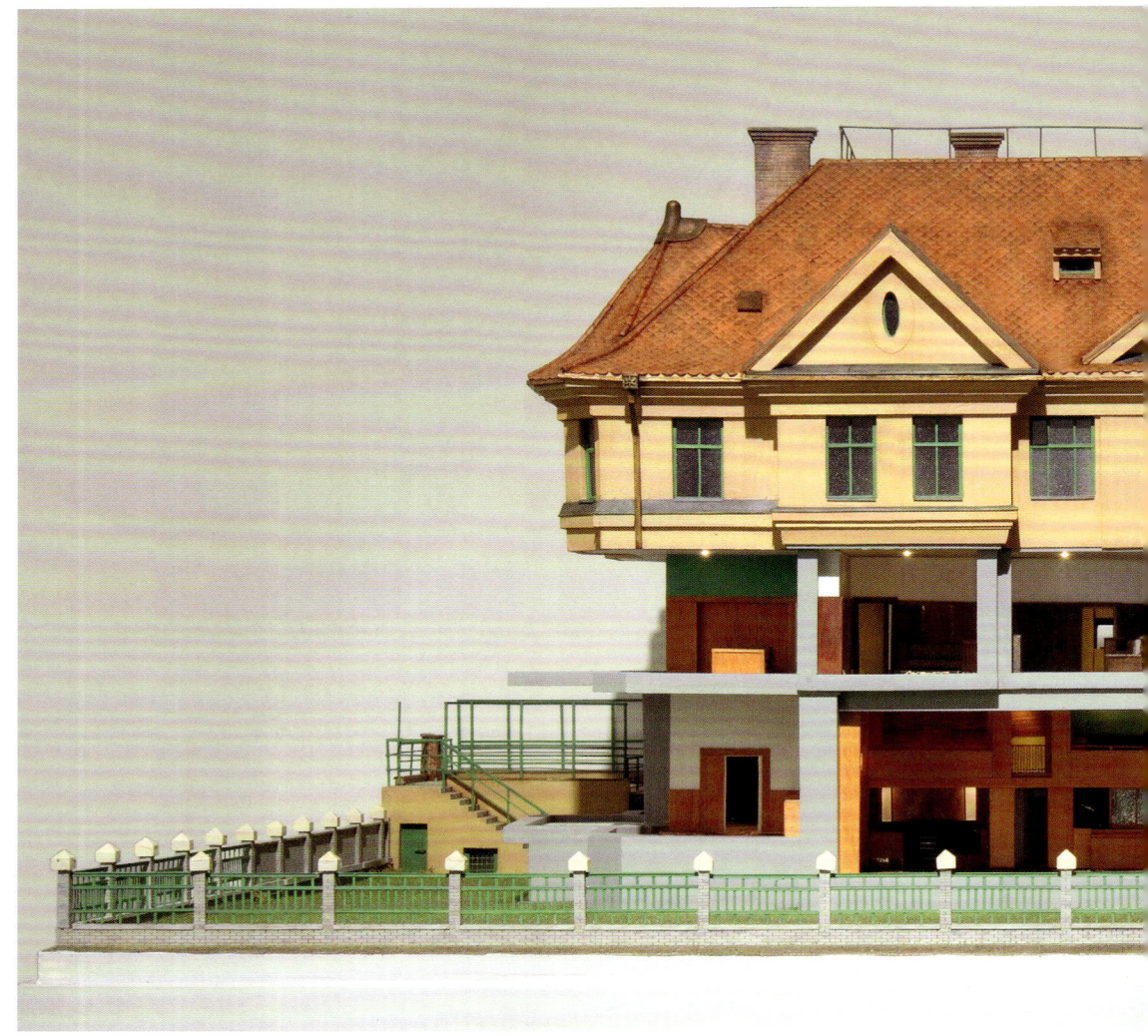

44/ A model of 110 Klatovská Avenue, Pilsen, with the apartment of Oskar Semler's family showing the situation in 1933–34; a view from the south, showing parts of the interior; model: Miroslav Koranda, 2021; photo: Karel Kocourek, 2022; ZČG

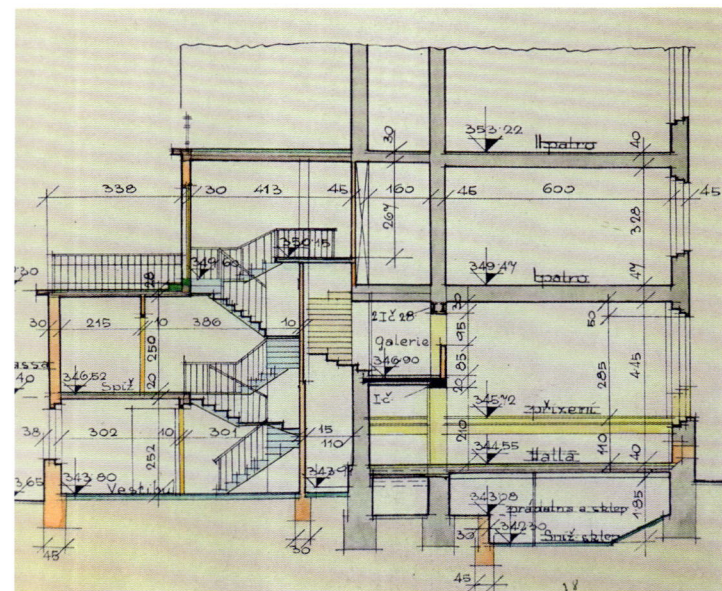

45/ A cross-section of Oskar Semler's family in 110 Klatovská Avenue, Pilsen, from the building project of the Müller & Kapsa company dated March 1933; the removal of vertical and horizontal structures (yellow) to create a large living hall (lounge) is visible; MMP, OSS; photo: Petr Domanický, 2021; ZČG

advance that the house they were buying was suitable for the intended purpose of building on the *Raumplan* principle. Therefore, unless (or until) new facts emerge, it should be appropriate, at a minimum, to continue to consider the concept of the Semler Residence the work of Kulka (and Krieger) as well as their mentor.

It is well documented that Heinrich Kulka stayed with Norbert Krieger in Pilsen at the turn of 1933, and we also know that he worked intensively on the plans for the reconstruction of part of the Semler Residence from January to early March 1933. Before the end of March, the Semlers applied for permission for the renovation and also for the construction of a garage adjacent to the house, and supported their application with a project similar to the one prepared by Kulka, but probably redrawn by someone at Müller & Kapsa. The actual construction began in July 1933 and ended in April of the following year. Approximately one year after the start of work, in July 1934, the Semlers moved into their new apartment. The modifications to the house and apartment were carried out by the Pilsen-based construction company Müller & Kapsa. The interior furnishings were supplied by the prestigious Prague furniture company of Emil Gerstel, which had furnished part of the Villa Müller in Prague. Atypical metal elements were made by Emanuel Velebil from Pilsen.

The modifications at the Semlers' included changes to the two existing apartments and part of the basement, as well as the addition of stairs, a conservatory and a new entrance, separated from the tenants' entrance. A major internal change was the creation of a two-storey lounge. The lounge was created in place of the three existing rooms of the first apartment, with the basement ceiling under their floor replaced by a new structure located more than a metre below the original ground floor. The replacement of its northern wall with a pair of pillars also connected the lounge visually and functionally with other rooms. The adjoining dining room and its facilities (kitchen and preparation room), as well as the guest room, remained at their original height and were connected to the lounge and to the gallery inserted into the lounge's upper part by flights of stairs. From the gallery, which is open to the lounge through three large windows, another floor of the apartment with rooms for family members and other facilities was connected by a single-flight staircase. This floor, which formed the sixth level of the spatial concept, was created by modifying the second of the original apartments and retained a separate direct entrance from the tenant's staircase. The centre of this floor is the upper 'yellow' hall.

The Semler family apartment occupies a substantial portion of the western half of the house (except for the top floor). The symmetrical northern façade originally faced the courtyard, which is in front of the main entrance. During the modification, small prismatic extensions were added in the right half containing a connecting staircase and a separate representative entrance leading to the new apartment. Together with the addition of a conservatory to the western façade and the enlargement of the windows in the southern façade, this intervention was one of the most significant changes to the external appearance of the house.

46/ The right side of the magazine spread with pictures of Paul Khuner's house in Payerbach and the Semler family apartment in Pilsen and the caption 'Im Geiste Adolf Loos' arbeitet sein Schüller Heinrich Kulka' ('Adolf Loos's pupil Heinrich Kulka works in the spirit of his teacher'); from: *Die Bühne*, 13.395 (1935), pp. 38–9

Behind the entrance there is a vestibule at the courtyard level with a glass skylight. The space has green walls and a floor of reddish ceramic tiles; the wall opposite the entrance is fitted with a large mirror. A small guest cloakroom follows at the front right-hand side, and a utility staircase is concealed behind a sliding door, providing staff with connections to all the main levels of the apartment. After descending the five travertine stairs, the symmetrical space of the large dressing room, originally also intended for guests, opens up at the level of the original basement.

At the end of the vestibule, five stairs above its level, the visitor enters the third level of the apartment. Here, after passing through a narrow corridor, the main living hall or lounge suddenly opens up. In contrast to the small entrance lobby, the hall impresses with its unexpected dimensions, which are further enhanced by its opening to other adjacent rooms, forming a whole with it, deliberately screened from the surroundings. These include the resting nooks on the gallery and below, the niche with the bar, but also the conservatory and the dining room, as well as the third level of the hall, which forms the core of the last, private floor of the apartment. The lounge space, almost 4.5 metres high, is composed along several axes. The longitudinal axis on one side points to a large fireplace flanked by greenish clinkstone blocks, while the opposite wall is dominated by a large Tibetan painting (now a reproduction), *The Life of Tsongkhapa*, depicting the life of a Tibetan Buddhist saint and teacher. The walls are panelled with Nordic birch (also known as Finnish or Karelian) veneer, while the parquet floor is veneered with Macassar ebony. A pair of transverse axes leads to two large sash windows in steel frames, equipped with opaque textured glass. Opposite one of the windows there is a niche with a bar tiled with black marble. Counterbalancing the other window is a resting nook with a gas fireplace, built-in benches in the style of a train compartment and an atypical light fixture made of a backlit slab of onyx-textured marble. The opposite window has a wide space between the inner and outer frames arranged like a greenhouse. The second resting area consists of armchairs of various shapes and styles, grouped directly in the lounge around a table placed in front of the large fireplace.

A short flight of stairs leads from the lounge to the mezzanine. Behind the sliding doors, which allow the space to be open to the hall, is the dining room, which is probably the most impressive space of the whole apartment. It has an octagonal ground plan, the walls are panelled with boards veneered with pyramid mahogany and the floor is made of boards veneered with wood known as 'citron' (also 'yellow satin' or 'satinwood') in the 1930s, which usually came from various tree species of

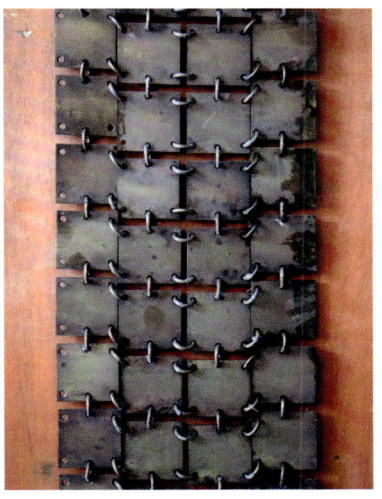

47/ A detail of the original thin partition above the dismantled wooden skin wall in the octagonal dining room of the flat at 110 Klatovská Avenue, Pilsen; photo: Petr Domanický, 2019; ZČG

48/ Part of the otherwise unpreserved decorative radiator cover from the front of the lounge; photo: Karel Kocourek, 2015; ZČG

Asia and America, some of which were unidentified at the time. The dining room is visually screened from the surroundings: the windows are covered by wooden frames with silk rectangles inserted between pairs of glass panes. Adjacent to the dining room is a conservatory, a guest room and a small washroom.

Another flight of stairs leads to the gallery that lines the upper part of the lounge opposite the windows. The gallery has a red beamed ceiling with gilded panels. The deeper part of the gallery, which also houses the dumb waiter, was used as a library. The shallower part of the gallery, equipped with a built-in sofa, was actually another resting nook. Between the two parts, the main transverse axis of the entire living space, directly above the entrance, opens onto a staircase leading to the upper 'yellow' hall, which was the hub of the private floor. This upper hall also has a separate entrance directly from the house staircase, which was frequently used by the family.

The central element of the upper 'yellow' hall is another resting nook, which also served as a small dining room. Behind this space, the most prominent part of this floor follows on with the rooms of Oskar and Jana Semler. Jana's room was located on the corner and is thus richly illuminated. It has built-in furniture and wall panelling veneered with maple in combination with walnut. In the cosy room

49/ A label of the carpentry supplier company *Emil Gerstel*; photo: Karel Kocourek, 2015; ZČG

there is a bed, made as a copy of the original, which has not survived. Oskar Semler's adjoining room has walls panelled with 'citron' veneer. The copy of the bed is embedded lengthwise in the niche, with a lamp from Emanuel Velebil's workshop in its original place. The wall opposite the window is dominated by a fireplace and a large mirror. The fireplace, equipped with an electric heater, has a white marble lining and a cover made of a series of glass tubes fitted in a brass frame. Between the two rooms there is a large bathroom, the present furnishing of which is again close to the original.

Another important group of rooms on the private floor comprises two children's rooms. The two younger siblings, Oldřich and Vilém, shared a room closer to their parents. The room is panelled in larch, with a pair of sofa-beds clamped between a pair of low cupboards, set into the corner opposite the windows. The adjoining room was occupied by Štěpán, the eldest of the three brothers. Opposite its entrance there is a built-in sofa-bed, which is supplemented by a copy of the original low glazed bookcase.

The upper 'yellow' hall is also connected to the service staircase, which connects the top floor of the apartment with its main entrance, but also with the lounge and kitchen facilities. The staircase is made of steel and its blue colour now corresponds to its original state, which was clarified by the restorer's research. At the dining room level, the kitchen facilities of the apartment are accessible from the staircase. They consist of the walk-through preparation room, which connects the kitchen not only with the service staircase but also directly to the dining room. The adjacent kitchen is equipped with the original built-in furniture and also an original double sink. Close to the kitchen and preparation room there is a pantry on the staircase mezzanine, where an electric refrigerator, similar in type to the original, is located in a niche.

Kulka and Krieger, working at the Semlers' on the implementation of the modifications, were not the only ones in Pilsen who had previously helped Loos with his work. As the city became the second focus of Loos's work after Vienna, a unique circle of collaborators formed around the famous architect. Many of them worked here independently during Loos's lifetime and also later. Some had deeper ties to the town: Kurt Unger and Ilse Günther had direct family connections here; Karel Lhota and Norbert Krieger lived here for many years; and Heinrich Kulka often stayed here for business reasons. Loos's Pilsen customers routinely approached his pupils and former colleagues at the end of his life or even after his death; therefore Kulka's work for Oskar Semler's family was no exception. For example, Samuel Teichner, for whom Loos, with Krieger's assistance, designed the interior of a dental surgery in Pilsen, subsequently had Kulka furnish his apartment and design a cottage in Špičák (Spitzberg) in the Bohemian Forest (Šumava), which was completed in 1936. A little later, Kulka similarly redesigned the house of the Hirsch family in Pilsen.

In 1938 Kulka moved from Vienna to East Bohemia, where he built a villa in Hronov and an apartment house in Hradec Králové in 1937–39. After the Nazi occupation of Czechoslovakia he emigrated to New Zealand and from 1940 worked in Auckland for the Fletcher Construction Company. He designed and completed dozens of buildings and from 1960 he worked as an independent architect, focusing his interest on designing houses. However, he never realised a design as spectacular as the Semler Residence in Pilsen, or another as distinctly 'Loosian'.

5. THE SEMLER FAMILY AND 'THEIR' HOUSES AFTER THE END OF THE FIRST CZECHOSLOVAK REPUBLIC

During the period when the Semler Residence was being built, dramatic events were changing Europe. When Adolf Loos died in August 1933 and at the same time major construction changes were taking place shaping the future form of the unique Pilsen residence of a prominent family, another Adolf – Hitler – had already held the position of Reich Chancellor in neighbouring Germany for several months. In the following year, when the Semlers moved into their new apartment, Hitler assumed the powers of the German president, civil war broke out in Austria and an attempted Nazi coup took place. The construction of the garage, which the family had envisaged from the beginning and which actually concluded the whole project, was completed on 14 March 1939. The next day, the German Nazi army occupied what was left of Czechoslovakia after the Munich Agreement of the

50/ Vilém (Will) Semler (left) came from Australia to visit his birthplace in summer 2014; photo: Karel Kocourek; ZČG

51/ A view from the terrace on the roof of the garage to the western façade of the house before the restoration began; photo: Petr Domanický, 2007; ZČG

previous September. Soon the gradual restriction of the normal life of the Jewish population began. In Pilsen the situation reached its peak in January 1942 with three transports, when more than 2,500 Jewish people were deported from the city. They went first to Terezín concentration camp and then to the extermination camps, from where less than a tenth of them returned after the war. Many of Loos's former Pilsen associates and customers, who were mostly Jewish, sought to emigrate. Krieger and Kulka left early, as did the Semlers, Hirschs and, in part, the Beck family. Claire (Klára) and other family members, however, did not succeed and lost their lives.

After the Second World War, most of the emigrants did not return, as the conditions were rather different from those before the war. On the contrary, after the Communists seized power in a coup in February 1948, the conditions were in many ways reminiscent of the wartime regime. The Semlers had settled in Australia: first their youngest son Vilém (Will) and then both parents, Oskar and Jana. Their departure was preceded by the forced surrender of their property to the Nazi occupiers. Similarly, the family of Oskar's brother Hugo left for Canada. Vilém's brother Oldřich went to the United States and served in the American army, Štěpán joined a Czechoslovak military brigade in Britain during the war, and his cousin Hanuš (Honza) served as a technician with the 311th Squadron of the Czechoslovak Air Force within the British RAF. The Semlers' properties in Pilsen, at 19 and 110 Klatovská Avenue, were officially taken over by the German Reich.

52/ A view from the conservatory and dining room to the lounge gallery with a reading nook, with the recent separation of the entrance (bottom right) and barred viewports (top right) to the lounge after the tenant had moved out; photo: Petr Domanický, 2009; ZČG

53/ A view from the upper 'yellow' hall into the corridor with built-in wardrobes; on the right, partially exposed original wallpaper and the place where the wall clock used to be; photo: Karel Kocourek, 2013; ZČG

54/ Jana Semler's room before restoration; an original bedside table (found elsewhere in the house) in the centre; photo: Karel Kocourek, 2013; ZČG

55/ The main lounge after the dismantling of the modern partition structures and after the start of the repair and restoration; photo: Karel Kocourek, 2015; ZČG

Like other houses and luxury apartments, they were to serve the institutions of the Nazi regime. The former became the seat of the German military headquarters, with the commander using the representative part of the former Hugo Semler family apartment. There, in May 1945, negotiations were held on the surrender of the German troops in Pilsen. The apartment of Oskar Semler's family was used in a similar way. According to the information given by his son Vilém (Will), the local headquarters of the *Luftwaffe* was located there. Oskar (Oscar) obtained a position in Australia as production manager in a wire and nail company and some of his inventions even received patent protection. With the help of a mortgage, the Semlers bought an older house in Melbourne. After the war, they set up their own business, trading in steel components and making various small metal items for other companies, as well as toys. After Oskar Semler had died in 1961, his wife Jana devoted herself to travelling. She outlived her husband by more than thirty years.

37/ Construction of the skylight above the glass ceiling in the vestibule during the repair; photo: Petr Domanický, 2015; ZČG

56/ Dismantled heavily damaged dining room wall panelling before restoration; photo: Petr Domanický, 2020; ZČG

After the war, the Semlers asked for the return of their two Pilsen houses; unfortunately, at that time Czechoslovakia was already ruled by the Communists without any democratic control. Neither of the families regained access to their property and the houses were declared confiscated. The house at number 110 was first owned by the city of Pilsen; in 1955 it was taken over by the state. The premises of the Semler family's apartment were used by the newly founded Pilsen Medical Faculty of the Charles University in Prague to house its dean's office, later a classroom and finally a warehouse for the school library. Already in 1959, the representative part of the apartment was fundamentally disrupted by separating and modifying the former guest room and the winter garden, used until then as offices. A small flat was created here, similar to the earlier private part, comprising the top floor of the Semlers' flat.

During the 1960s, several Czech experts became interested in the work of Adolf Loos. In 1968, when a certain 'democratisation' of Communism was at its peak in Czechoslovakia, the conservationist Věra Běhalová documented the preserved Loosian interiors of Pilsen, which subsequently, including the former apartment of the Semler family, were listed as moveable heritage monuments. Although the protection mostly prevented the complete destruction of the interiors, it was not able to stop their gradual decline.

It was only after the changes initiated in Czechoslovakia in November 1989 by the Velvet Revolution that the restoration of the democratic system in the country, which was soon divided into the independent Czech and Slovak Republics, began. Vilém (Will) Semler and his wife Gwen visited Pilsen in 1991 for the first time since 1939. However, the family did not seek the return of their property. The house again became the property of the city of Pilsen; the former apartment remained divided into small residential units and the lounge was home to a private photo studio. From the early 1990s onwards Pilsen's expert conservation organisation (now the National Heritage Institute) took an interest in the architecture of the first half of the twentieth century, which until then had been almost completely neglected in Pilsen. The interest in the surviving Loos-related works deepened after the completion of the restoration of Prague's Villa Müller, which was followed after 2000 by several promotional events related to Pilsen, the beginning of the restoration of the Brummel House, which was reclaimed by the family, and the city's first activities aimed at rehabilitating the Loos legacy.

58/ Built-in cabinet and the reverse of the dining-room wall panel before the refurbishment was completed and fitted back into its original location; photo: Petr Domanický, 2021; ZČG

59/ Restoration works on the plaster of the western façade of the house; photo: Petr Domanický, 2021; ZČG

6. RESTORATION OF THE SEMLER RESIDENCE IN 2012–23

Welcome to the Semler Residence. You can leave your coats in the downstairs cloakroom, then go straight ahead, turn right and you will be greeted by my ghost in the lounge.

Vilém (Will) Semler: a message to visitors in an email to the author dated 18 December 2022

Two publications in 2009 (Maria Szadkowska et al., *Adolf Loos: The Work of Adolf Loos in the Czech Lands*, and Petr Urlich (ed.), *Slavné vily Plzeňského kraje*) marked an important milestone for the Semler Residence and the Gallery of West Bohemia in Pilsen (GWB), where the sub-collection of architecture had just been established. In the same year GWB conducted its first inspection of the apartment and began to consider its possible acquisition. Two years later, the gallery organised a large exhibition project focusing on Adolf Loos and his work in Pilsen (*Loos – Plzeň – Souvislosti / Loos – Pilsen – Connections*), with an emphasis on recalling the hitherto almost unknown fates of the families of the former private investors in architectural commissions. At that time, the gallery established cooperation with Vilém (Will) Semler, who lives in Australia, and the exhibition was visited by Loos's niece Janet Beck Wilson from Great Britain and nephew Charles Paterson from the USA. A key decision was made in 2012, when, as a result of the GWB's interest, the city of Pilsen, after a series of negotiations initiated on behalf of the gallery by its director Roman Musil, transferred the entire Semler Residence to the ownership of the Pilsen Region, which is the founding authority of the gallery.

After detailed preparation, work began on the gradual restoration of the house. Given the limited financial possibilities, two less extensive parts of the restoration were carried out in 2013–15, focusing on solving the most urgent problems, such as the reconstruction of the dilapidated flat roofs and the heating and restoration of the most damaged interiors. In the process, the spatial logic of the entire historic interior was restored after decades, the entrance area and conservatory were reconstructed, and the heavily damaged cloakrooms were repaired. In 2015, when Pilsen was the European Capital of Culture, a substantial part of the historic interior opened to the public. Before that, in the summer of 2014, members of Hugo

60/ General view of the restored Semler Residence from the south-west; photo: Radovan Kodera, 2023; ZČG

61/ Entrance to the apartment and the main entrance to the house (left) in the northern façade of the restored house; photo: Petr Polák, 2022; ZČG

62/ Entrance vestibule of the apartment after the completion of the renovations; access to the lounge follows to the right at the rear; photo: Radovan Kodera, 2023; ZČG

and Oskar Semler's families had visited Pilsen, including the then ninety-year-old Vilém (Will) Semler, Oskar's youngest son.

    The key to further progress was the successful application for a subsidy from the European Union's Integrated Regional Operational Programme, intended mainly for restoration work, ensuring barrier-free operation of part of the house and the establishment of an expert centre for architectural research. In addition, the Pilsen Region provided further funds and decided that the entire implementation would be completed in the next stage. In 2019–21 the company SILBA-Elstav and its collaborators, which included a number of restorers specialising in various crafts, carried out the decisive stage of the works. These were based, as in the previous phase, on a project prepared by Projektový atelier pro architekturu a pozemní stavby (Project studio for architecture and civil engineering; the team of architect Tomáš Šantavý from Prague). The initial study was prepared by architect Radek Dragoun from Pilsen, the interiors of the new premises and some other modifications were designed by Veselák+Toman architekti (Pilsen). For the restoration of the historic interior, the expert input of the GWB itself was indispensable. The gallery's representative refined the solution by, among other things, preparing the documents and consulting with the restorers and Vilém (Will) Semler, as well as selecting many elements, all in an effort to preserve the authenticity and restore the unique atmosphere. The work carried out included the almost complete repair and adaptation of the house, the landscaping of the surrounding grounds and, in particular, the almost complete restoration of the historic interior as well as the façades. In the eastern part of the house, three small apartments, a visitor information centre with space for educational programmes, a multi-purpose hall and meeting rooms and a depository for the architecture collection were created. An important contribution to the popularisation of the rehabilitated heritage monument was the opening of the Café Semler in the elevated basement of the house. In addition to its regular operation, the café also hosts some of the GWB's chamber events.

The historical interior is complemented by exhibitions focusing on the Semler family, Adolf Loos and the architecture of Pilsen in the years 1874–1939. In addition to text panels, they offer documentary videos, photo albums with reproductions of historical photographs and several architectural models of important Pilsen buildings; a notable curiosity is the preserved writing desk of Loos's collaborator Karel Lhota from his Pilsen apartment.

The entire repair of the house was observed with great attention and interest from Melbourne by Vilém (Will) Semler, who was kept informed by the author of this book, who supervised the work on behalf of the GWB. When the building opened to the public on 19 September 2022, with the participation of the Minister of Culture of the Czech Republic, Martin Baxa, the Governor of the Pilsen Region, Rudolf Špoták, and many other guests, Vilém (Will) Semler sent a greeting and a message for the occasion, which included some humorous memories of his childhood in the house and a greeting:

> *Enjoy the tour; you can imagine all the funny things that used to happen in this architectural novelty, like the dog who, instead of barking when someone opened the door, fell asleep every time … All the best and ahoy!*
>
> *Vilouš Semler*

65/ The restored service staircase; photo: Petr Polák, 2022; ZČG

64/ The renovated washroom by the large guest cloakroom; photo: Radovan Kodera, 2023; ZČG

At the beginning of December 2022 the café opened for the public, which further expanded the facilities for visitors, until then consisting mainly of the information centre. The interiors of this part of the building have a contemporary architectural concept, which, however, creatively relates to the valuable earlier stages of the building's development.

In 2023 the repository of the architectural collection began operation and the new multi-purpose hall for cultural events and conferences was finally equipped with funds from the Pilsen Region. The exhibition in the historic interior was enriched by a newly created replica of the built-in furniture in the guest room. In the spring of that year, the Semler Residence became one of the most famous modernist houses registered in the Iconic Houses network, and as soon as May, several dozen experts from various countries visited the residence as part of the *Icons of the Czech Avant-Garde* conference. Janet Beck Wilson from Great Britain, the niece of Claire (Klára) Loos, and later Hannah and Anita Semler from Australia, granddaughters of Oskar and Jana Semler, also came to visit the site. In September, the jury of the Pilsen Region Building of the Year competition awarded the restoration of the Semler Residence with the Jury Prize, and in November, the GWB published a detailed book about the Semler Residence, whose patrons were Prof. Christopher Long, a leading Loosian scholar and professor at the University of Texas at Austin, and Prof. Rostislav Švácha, a renowned Czech architectural historian. The publication was dedicated to Vilém (Will) Semler, who celebrated his hundredth birthday in November 2023.

65/ The laundry room after renovation; photo: Radovan Kodera, 2023; ZČG

66/ The large guest cloakroom after restoration, a view from the entrance; photo: Radovan Kodera, 2023; ZČG

67/ Entrance from the vestibule to the lounge after renovation; photo: Petr Polák, 2022; ZČG

68/ The lounge after restoration;
photo: Radovan Kodera, 2023; ZČG

69/ The north wall of the lounge with gallery; below is the restored resting nook; photo: Radovan Kodera, 2023; ZČG

70/ The library in the extended part of the gallery above the lounge; photo: Radovan Kodera, 2023; ZČG

71/ General view of the lounge from the gallery; photo: Radovan Kodera, 2023; ZČG

72/ A view from the resting nook at the lounge gallery towards the conservatory; photo: Radovan Kodera, 2023; ZČG

73/ A view from the restored dining room and conservatory to the lounge gallery; photo: Radovan Kodera, 2023; ZČG

74/ A view from the conservatory to the guest room and lounge; photo: Radovan Kodera, 2023; ZČG

75/ The conservatory after its renovation; photo: Radovan Kodera, 2023; ZČG

76/ A view from the dining room after its restoration to the preparation room and to the service staircase; photo: Petr Polák, 2022; ZČG

77/ A view through the preparation room by the kitchen towards the service staircase from the dining room; photo: Radovan Kodera, 2023; ZČG

78/ General view of the kitchen after restoration; photo: Radovan Kodera, 2023; ZČG

79/ Part of the preparation room at the entrance from the service staircase after restoration; photo: Petr Polák, 2022; ZČG

80/ Pantry by the service staircase and kitchen after renovation and furnishing with a historic electric refrigerator; photo: Radovan Kodera, 2023; ZČG

81/ The staircase connecting the gallery of the lounge and the upper 'yellow' hall after restoration; photo: Radovan Kodera, 2022; ZČG

82/ The restored upper 'yellow' hall with a resting nook and access to the main house staircase; photo: Radovan Kodera, 2023; ZČG

83/ Oskar Semler's room after restoration;
photo: Radovan Kodera, 2023; ZČG

THE SEMLER RESIDENCE

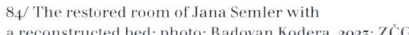
84/ The restored room of Jana Semler with a reconstructed bed; photo: Radovan Kodera, 2023; ZČG

85/ The restored bathroom between Oskar and Jana Semler's rooms; photo: Radovan Kodera, 2023; ZČG

THE SEMLER RESIDENCE

This edition © B. T. Batsford Ltd., 2024
Text and illustrations © The Gallery of West Bohemia in Pilsen, 2024

First published in 2024
Scala Arts & Heritage Publishers Ltd
43 Great Ormond Street
London WC1N 3HZ
United Kingdom
www.scalapublishers.com
An imprint of B. T. Batsford Holdings Ltd.

In association with the Gallery of West Bohemia in Pilsen
Pražská 13, 301 00 Pilsen, Czech Republic
www.zpc-galerie.cz

ISBN: 978-1-78551-459-3

Project managers: Kateřina Siegl, Beth Holmes (Scala) and Tomáš Hausner (GWB)
Author: Petr Domanický
Introduction: Christopher Long
Translation: Tomáš Hausner and Connaire Haggan
Language editing: First Edition Translations Ltd, Cambridge
Graphic Design: Bušek+Dienstbier

Printed and bound in Turkey

10 9 8 7 6 5 4 3 2 1

All rights reserved. No part of this book may be reproduced, stored in a retrieval system or transmitted in any form or by any means, electronic, mechanical, photocopying, recording or otherwise, without the written permission of the Gallery of West Bohemia in Pilsen and Scala Arts & Heritage Publishers Ltd.

The Semler Residence
Západočeská galerie v Plzni, p. o.
Klatovská třída č. 110
301 00 Pilsen, Czech Republic
email: info@semler.cz
tel.: + 420 770 131 810
www.semler.cz, www.zpc-galerie.cz

FRONT COVER:
A view of the lounge after restoration; photo: Petr Polák 2022; ZČG

BACK COVER:
Upper 'yellow' hall and stairs descending to the gallery of the lounge; photo: Petr Polák 2022; ZČG

FRONT FLAP:
An overall view of the Semler Residence after restoration; photo: Petr Polák 2022; ZČG

BACK FLAP:
The author; photo: Tomáš Kárník 2024; ZČG

PP. 2–3
A view along Klatovská Avenue in Pilsen from the centre. In the middle is number 19, where Oskar and Jana Semler were planning an extension. Postcard, c.1927; collection (archive) of the author

P. 4
A view from the gallery into the main space of the lounge; photo: Petr Polák 2022; ZČG

P. 118
A detail of the built-in dressing table in Jana Semler's room; photo: Petr Polák 2022; ZČG

Photographs and Reproductions

ALBERTINA Museum, Wien (6, Bruno Reiffenstein 7, Martin Gerlach ml. 20); Archiv města Plzně (9, 28, 41); G-Team Holding SE, závod Vochov (29); Magistrát města Plzně, technický úřad, odbor stavebně správní (45); Muzeum literatury – Památník národního písemnictví, Literární archiv (11); sbírka (archiv) Viléma (Willa) Semlera (34, 36); Státní oblastní archiv v Plzni (14, 43); Uměleckoprůmyslové museum v Praze (16, 17, 19, Atelier Pařík 18); Západočeská galerie v Plzni (22, Petr Domanický 1, 10, 21, 24, 25, 32, 33, 35, 38, 42, 45, 47, 51, 52, 56, 57, 58, 59, Josef Hanuš [?] 4, 12, Tomáš Kárník cover, Karel Kocourek 39, 44, 48, 49, 50, 53, 54, 55, Radovan Kodera 13, 27, 37, 60, 62, 64, 65, 66, 68, 69, 70, 71, 72, 73, 74, 75, 77, 78, 80, 81, 82, 83, 84, 85, 86, 87, 88, 89, 90 Karel Lhota [?] 5, 8, Oto Palán 15, Petr Polák 61, 63, 67, 76, 79, cover); Západočeské muzeum v Plzni, národopisné oddělení (30, Atelier Carl Pietzner, 26).

Drawings

Patricie Císlerová (3, 23), Petr Domanický (40), Bušek+Dienstbier (maps)

Articles

- BĚHALOVÁ, Věra, 'Pilsner Wohnungen von Adolf Loos', *Bauforum*, 3.21 (1970), pp. 49–56
- BĚHALOVÁ, Věra, 'Beitrag zu einer Kulka-Forschung', *Bauforum*, 7.43 (1974), pp. 22–31
- HUČKA, Jan, 'Železářská továrna Š. Semlera', in HLUŠIČKOVÁ, Hana (ed.), *Technické památky v Čechách, na Moravě a ve Slezsku IV*, Praha 2004, pp. 179–80
- KUDĚLKA, Zdeněk, 'Činnost Adolfa Loose v Československu', *Sborník prací Filosofické fakulty brněnské university*, 22, F 17, Brno 1973, pp. 141–55
- KUDĚLKA, Zdeněk, 'Činnost Adolfa Loose v Československu II', *Sborník prací Filosofické fakulty brněnské university*, 23, F 18, Brno 1974, pp. 7–32
- KURRENT, Friedrich, 'Loos, Hoffmann and My Generation', in THUN-HOHENSTEIN, Christoph, BOECKL, Matthias, and WITT-DÖRRING, Christian (eds), *Josef Hoffmann, Adolf Loos: Ways to Modernism and Their Impact*, Basel 2015, pp. 259–61
- LHOTA, Karel, 'Architekt A. Loos', *Architekt SIA*, 32 1933, pp. 137–43
- ŠVÁCHA, Rostislav, 'Adolf Loos a česká architektura', *Umění*, 31.6, 1983, pp. 490–512

Illustration Sources

- ALA: ALBERTINA Museum, Vienna, fund (estate) ALA (Adolf-Loos-Archiv)
- AMP: (Archiv města Plzně / Pilsen Municipal Archives), library, maps and plans collection, photography collection
- G-Team Holding SE Company Archives, Vochov plant
- LA ML–PNP: (Literární archiv Muzea literatury – Památníku národního písemnictví / Museum of Czech Literature, Literary Archive), fund (estate) of Jaromír John
- MMP, OSS: (Magistrát města Plzně, technický úřad, odbor stavebně správní – spisovna / Municipal Authorities of the City of Pilsen, Technical Office, Building Administration Department – Record Office) – building file k. 721 J
- SVK PK: (Studijní a vědecká knihovna Plzeňského kraje / Education and Research Library of the Region of Pilsen)
- SOA v Plzni: (Státní oblastní archiv v Plzni / State Regional Archives in Pilsen), Office Klášter, fund Škoda Plzeň, Photographic Documentation
- UPM: (Uměleckoprůmyslové museum v Praze / Museum of Decorative Arts in Prague), fund (estate) of Milada Müllerová
- ZČG: (Západočeská galerie v Plzni / Gallery of West Bohemia in Pilsen), Architecture Collection, Archives
- ZČM, NO: (Západočeské muzeum v Plzni, národopisné oddělení / Museum of West Bohemia in Pilsen, Ethnography Department), Collection of Photography and Negatives
- ZČM, OND: (Západočeské muzeum v Plzni, oddělení novějších dějin / Museum of West Bohemia in Pilsen, Modern History Department), Collection of Photography and Negatives
- Other publications, periodicals and the private collections (archives) of Vilém (Will) Semler and the author

8. SELECT BIBLIOGRAPHY

Books

- ALTMANN-LOOS, Elsie, *Mein Leben mit Adolf Loos*, Wien 2013
- ARTARIA, Paul, *Ferien- und Landhäuser / Weekend- and Country-Houses*, Erlenbach, Zürich 1947
- BECK-LOOS, Claire, *ADOLF LOOS: A Private Portrait*, s.l. 2011
- CHADRABA, Rudolf, KRULICHOVÁ, Marie, and VINAŘOVÁ, Milena (eds), *Bohumil Markalous: Estetika praktického života*, Praha 1989
- CHATRNÝ, Jindřich, and ČERNOUŠKOVÁ, Dagmar (eds), *Brněnské stopy Adolfa Loose*, Brno 2010
- DOMANICKÝ, Petr, *Pracovna republiky: Architektura Plzně v letech 1918–1938*, Plzeň 2018
- DOMANICKÝ, Petr, *Semlerova rezidence v Plzni: Trojrozměrný příběh Adolfa Loose a Heinricha Kulky*, Plzeň 2023
- DOMANICKÝ, Petr, and JINDRA, Petr (eds), *Loos – Plzeň – souvislosti / Loos – Pilsen – Connections*, Plzeň 2011
- FRAMPTON, Kenneth, *Modern Architecture: A Critical History*, London 2020
- GAUDIN, Mary, and REID, Giles, *Henry Kulka*, London 2022
- GÖSSEL, Gabriel (ed.), *SEM*, Praha 2018
- HUBATOVÁ-VACKOVÁ, Lada, and NIKOLENKO, Valentyna (eds), *Vila Jenny a Josefa Winternitzových*, Praha 2020
- JIROUT, František, *Dřevo v přírodě a řemeslech, v živnosti a průmyslu vůbec (II)*, Praha 1928
- KOULA, Jan E., *Nová česká architektura a její vývoj ve XX. století*, Praha 1940
- KRISTAN, Markus (ed.), *Adolf Loos: Wohnungen*, Wien 2001
- KSANDR, Karel (ed.), *Müllerova vila*, Praha, 2000
- KULKA, Heinrich, *Adolf Loos: Das Werk des Architekten*, Wien 1931
- LONG, Christopher, *Adolf Loos: Poslední domy / The Last Houses*, Praha 2020
- LONG, Christopher, *Adolf Loos on Trial*, Brno 2017
- LOOS, Adolf, *Spoken into the Void: Collected Essays 1897–1900*, Cambridge, MA, 1987
- LOOS, Lina, *Das Buch ohne Titel: Erlebte Geschichten*, Wien 2015
- PATERSON, Charles, and PATERSON, Carrie, *Escape Home: Rebuilding a Life after the Anschluss. A Family Memoir*, Los Angeles 2013
- PETR, František, and KOSTKA, Jiří: *Městské památkové reservace v Čechách a na Moravě*, Praha 1955
- RISSELADA, Max (ed.), *Raumplan versus Plan libre: Adolf Loos / Le Corbusier*, Zlín, 2012
- RUKSCHCIO, Burkhard, and SCHACHEL, Roland, *Adolf Loos, Leben und Werk*, Salzburg, Wien 1982
- SARNITZ, August, *Adolf Loos*, Praha 2004
- SEMLER, Will, *The Family Paper Weight*, Melbourne s.d.
- SVOBODA, Petr, and ŠOLC Martin, *Následovníci Adolfa Loose: Práce v českých zemích*, Brno, 2020
- SZADKOWSKA, Maria (ed.), *Adolf Loos, Dílo a rekonstrukce, Mezinárodní sympozium u příležitosti 70. výročí úmrtí, Plzeň 15.–16. října 2003*, Praha 2005
- SZADKOWSKA, Maria, VAN DUZER, Leslie, and ČERNOUŠKOVÁ, Dagmar, *Adolf Loos – dílo v českých zemích*, Praha 2009
- ŠLAPETA, Vladimír (ed.), *Adolf Loos a česká architektura*, exhibition catalogue, s. l., s. d. [1984]
- URLICH, Petr (ed.), *Slavné vily Plzeňského kraje*, Praha 2009
- WASKA, Karel (ed.), *Dějiny města Plzně 2: 1788–1918*, Plzeň 2016

Pilsen is of exceptional value in this respect, as the monument saved, restored and made accessible has a significance that goes beyond the borders of the region and the Czech Republic. It is an almost unknown building, representing in a way the culmination of the unique activity of Adolf Loos and his circle in the Czech lands.

The GWB is following the repair of the house and the restoration of the historic interior with other professional activities related to the architecture of south-west Bohemia at the end of the nineteenth century and the first half of the twentieth century. This mainly involves research work and the subsequent presentation of its outcomes in the form of exhibitions and publications. In addition to the events held in Pilsen, the gallery has also prepared an exhibition entitled *Loos and Pilsen*, which the Czech Centres, established by the Czech Ministry of Foreign Affairs, have presented since 2020 (the 150th anniversary of Loos's birth) in Tel Aviv, New York, Vienna, Paris, Brussels and Tokyo. The exhibition returned to Pilsen in 2023 (quite fittingly and symbolically, the ninetieth anniversary of the architect's death), where it was made available in an updated form in the historic city hall.

7. CONCLUSION

The Czech Republic is very rich in architectural monuments from the Middle Ages, Renaissance and Baroque eras. However, equally outstanding buildings also come from the nineteenth and the first half of the twentieth centuries, particularly the inter-war period, when Czechia and Slovakia were part of advanced, democratic Czechoslovakia. It was a characteristic of this period that, alongside a surprising number of exceptional architectural gems in the major centres, high standards were commonplace in smaller towns and less prominent regions. In addition to such icons as the renovation of Prague Castle, the founding of new districts in Prague and the construction of individual outstanding buildings, the cities and towns of Hradec Králové, Brno and Zlín were transformed. At the same time, excellent technical infrastructure, schools, sports facilities, residential districts and entire urban complexes were created, for example, in the cities of North Bohemia, Slovakia and Ruthenia, and even quite commonly in the countryside.

Pilsen, located less than a hundred kilometres south-west of Prague, has long been one of the most important Czech cities. Since the second half of the nineteenth century it has been transformed into one of the Central European centres of industry. This led to prosperity and generous projects, but architecturally and, above all, urbanistically, the rapidly expanding city lagged behind contemporary developments. The exception was construction initiated by individuals, which often went far beyond the borders of the region. Since around 1910 and especially during the inter-war period, however, the overall situation changed positively. In addition to improving the quality of new public buildings and new quarters, the municipality began to work towards the gradual restoration of existing neighbourhoods, which had largely been created in the nineteenth century.

The unique development and transformation of Pilsen and the whole country was tragically affected by the Second World War, after which the direction of the country changed significantly, a fate sealed by the Communist coup in February 1948. In terms of urban planning, Pilsen moved towards radical reconstruction, which, however, under the conditions of the regime of the time, led to serious damage to the structure and appearance of the city as a whole, especially its centre. Only after the re-establishment of democracy and the integration of the republic into European structures after 1989 did the approach to the urban environment slowly change. One of the most visible positive results since then has been the preservation of numerous monuments. The restoration of the Semler Residence in

90/ The café's new logo, located on the main façade of the building, is made using classic neon-tube technology and its shape is reminiscent of the historical trademark *Sem*; photo: Radovan Kodera, 2023; ZČG

89/ Café Semler, adjacent to the visitor centre, was built on the premises of the former caretaker's flat and the adjacent cellar in the raised basement; photo: Radovan Kodera, 2023; ZČG

88/ The new visitor centre on the raised ground floor of the eastern part of the house; photo: Radovan Kodera, 2023; ZČG

THE SEMLER RESIDENCE

87/ Exposition of the architecture of Pilsen at the end of the nineteenth and the beginning of the twentieth century, located in the former governess's room; the desk on display comes from the apartment of the architect Karel Lhota, where the project of the Villa Müller was drafted; photo: Radovan Kodera, 2023; ZČG

86/ A view from the children's room of Vilém (Will) and Oldřich to the room of Štěpán Semler, in both cases after restoration and addition of missing details; photo: Radovan Kodera, 2023; ZČG